Sept. 2008

D0091899

Brad –

Thank you for your willingness. help me with this bo project. I so much apprec your time and your kind words. In your business may you enjoy "your financial" journey)!

Renee

What Others Are Saying...

"*Your Financial Flight Plan* contains essential nuggets of wisdom and components of how a business can run more smoothly and more profitably. Throughout the book, Renee has placed ways to check and make improvements in your business. This small volume is worth the read, even if you think you know everything there is to know about business."
Casey Dawes, Wise Women Shining, www.wisewomenshining.com

"Renee Daggett offers essential financial management insights for small business owners who want their business to soar to new heights."
Kevin W. McCarthy, Author of *The On-Purpose Business*, CEO of On Purpose Business Advisors, www.on-purpose.com

"If there's a better analogy for running a business than flying a plane, I can't think what it would be. The ideas Ms. Daggett presents come from knowledge gained from working with many businesses and their CEOs. The effectiveness of her methods has been proven over and over again."
Alyson Hamilton, Intuit, Small Business Division, www.intuit.com

"This effort by Renee is long overdue. As a tax professional, the chapters on financial statements are important to the success of any business."
Chuck Doubleday, Enrolled Agent, www.doubledaytax.com

"*Your Financial Flight Plan* is a must read for business owners who find themselves pulled in a million directions. Renee has taken the time to make extremely important and sometimes confusing concepts clear through engaging exercises. This book provides the indispensable building blocks for a strong company!"
Charles N. Vezinaw, Managing Director of Merchant Support Network, Inc., www.merchantsupport.com

"The idea of relating the running of a business to flying a plane is a stroke of genius. If these practices are followed, any business person will be successful."

Ken Edwards, Charter Officer of Mt. Diablo Pilots Association & Aircraft Sales Owner

"It is a wonder that there is not more information like this book pointed in the direction of day-to-day management of small businesses. This book offers a simple yet concise explanation of the financial aspects of business, allowing the reader insight. Reading this book is a great start for all business owners seeking information on running a business in today's marketplace."

Sandra Hunter-Ferris, Senior Vice President & SBA Department Manager of Pinnacle Bank, www.pinnaclebankonline.com

"*Your Financial Flight Plan* is a must read for business owners who are serious about taking action and seeing results. Renee explains practical business basics using aviation analogies that are entertaining, creative and effective."

Kimberly Fulcher, CEO of MyLifeCompass and Author of *Remodel Your Reality*, www.mylifecompass.com

"*Your Financial Flight Plan* does an outstanding job of helping business owners understand the importance of money management and leadership. It is engaging and very practical…just what busy entrepreneurs need. Every CEO will profit from reading this excellent book!!"

Howard Dayton, Cofounder of Crown Financial Ministries and Author of Your Money Counts, www.crown.org

"By reading this book, business owners will improve their understanding of how they can become more effective business managers. The business advice is sound and owners of medium and small businesses would benefit from reading it. The aviation analogies are accurate and made the book interesting to read."

Mark Sochan, President of the South County Airport Pilots Association, www.southcountypilots.org

"I am thrilled with how simple and easy you made it for the small (or large) business owner to get these critical concepts. The short, simple explanations of the topics and the flying analogies, followed by the action steps, make this the perfect "getting started" tool. How incredible it would be if every new business owner read this great book before starting their business. I intend to use it to help the small business owners I counsel every week. Great job!"

   **Rick Siebert, Founder & President of Cornerstone Credit
   Counseling**

"Renee has written an excellent operating manual for business owners (and pilots) who want to execute their vision skillfully. With weaving experience and wisdom into the analogy of aviation makes this book both informative and thought provoking. Flying airplanes and running a business must be taken seriously if we want to arrive at the proper destination, and *Your Financial Flight Plan* gives us practical guidelines to enjoy the journey while arriving in style."

   **Sung Cho, Pilot for a Major U.S. airline and Co-Founder and
   Dad of Van Beek Kids, www.vanbeekkids.com**

"*Your Financial Flight Plan*" is neither fluff nor a silly analogy. Renee's book is full of down to earth common sense knowledge for small business people. If you read this book, your chances of success will be much higher. Those who are thinking about going into business should read this book. And those who are in business should use the book as a reminder of sound business practices and to brush up on their everyday skills. No fluff, just good solid advice from someone who obviously has been around the "business block."

   **Brad Jones, President of BookSmart Enterprises, Inc.,
   www.mybooksmart.com**

"*Your Financial Flight Plan* is a great introduction to finances, corporate benefits and responsibilities, cash flow, business management and profitability for all small business owners."

   **Alexis Martin Neely, Personal Family Lawyer, Founder of the
   Family Wealth Planning Institute and Author of the bestselling
   *Wear Clean Underwear: A Fast, Fun, Friendly—and
   Essential—Guide to Legal Planning for Busy Parents*,
   www.PersonalFamilyLawyer.com**

"Every business owner needs to follow through with Renee's suggestions in the book because it is an invaluable resource for managing your small business."

**Kristy Rogers, Executive Managing Director of
eWomen Network San Jose,
www.ewomennetwork.com/chapter/sanjose**

"Renee has given a refreshing twist to a subject that has been covered at least thousands, if not tens of thousands of times. The successful use of the Airline Captain analogy to the CEO of a business gives the book a certain sizzle, and at the same time offers a "Flight Plan" that is at once both genuine and on target; an achievement where many similar efforts on this popular theme ("how to run a business") seem too often to fall short.

**Richard Fitzgerald, Rear Admiral, USNR (Retired),
Commercial Airline Pilot, (Retired)**

Your Financial Flight Plan

Pilot Your Business To Profitability

Renee Daggett

Your Financial Flight Plan: Pilot Your Business To Profitability

This publication is designed to provide general information regarding the subject matter covered. However, laws and practices often vary from state to state and are subject to change. Because each situation is different, specific advice should be tailored to the particular circumstances. For this reason, the reader is advised to consult with his or her own advisor regarding their specific situation.

The author and publisher have taken reasonable precautions in the preparation of this book and believe the facts presented are accurate as of the date it was written. However, neither the author nor the publisher assumes any responsibility for any errors or omissions. The author and publisher specifically disclaim any liability resulting from the use or application of the information contained in this book. The information is not intended to serve as legal, financial or other professional advice related to individual or business situations.

ISBN: 978-0-9820683-9-7

Additional copies of this book are available at www.yourfinancialflightplan.com or by contacting inquiry@yourfinancialflightplan.com

Copyeditor: Lynette Smith, All My Best
Book Cover Design: Lisa Liddy, The Printed Page

Presented by Renee Daggett and Admin Books:

Admin Books
1-888-459-1110
www.adminbooks.com

Contents

Acknowledgments

Had it not been for the encouragement and support of my husband, Doug, I would not be in this place. Because of his belief in my abilities, I have been able to fulfill a calling that goes beyond my own life. His countless selfless acts have given me the opportunity to grow. I will always strive to make sure he is honored at the gate.

Thank you to Larry Carr, a retired Navy pilot and 21-year Captain for American Airlines. You have provided me with many stories and educated me on aviation. I hope you will be pleased with how the interviews came together.

Thank you to Steve Nation and Gerald Kerr for reviewing my aviation and business analogies, sharing your insights and brainstorming with me.

A special tribute goes to my parents, Dick and JoAn Geistert, who have always loved me unconditionally.

God, I am not sure what you will do with this. I pray that Your message is heard. May the written words and insight expressed glorify Your name! Thank you for allowing me to be a part of Your work.

To Andrew and Ryan, you are my joy. I hope that what you read will motivate you to excellence in whatever you do in life!

Introduction

Close your eyes. Can you see it? Freedom. Peace. Contentment.

Take a deep breath. In your mind's eye, picture what your business looks like 3 years, 5 years, 10 years from now. Where are you standing? Who is around you? What do you hear? And how do you feel?

If you are a typical business owner, you are pulled in many directions. You must know about sales, marketing, research, accounting, human resources ... the list goes on. And you are exhausted. Many people give up. It's tough being a business owner, isn't it?

So why do so many travel down the road of entrepreneurship? More flexible hours? Not having to punch a time clock? To be your own boss? Maybe. The most important question is, Why are you a business owner? Have you ever taken the time to articulate the reason you do what you do?

When you know why you are in business, you have the fire and motivation to do it right. We all need a sense of purpose. Each person is created with talent. If we use that talent, it will fulfill us. Having a business filled with purpose

1

goes far beyond our immediate and selfish desires. This purpose adds something more to our life.

My own journey started in 1995 when my husband told me he was going to start his own business. My first reaction was, "No way!" Thankfully, he did not listen to me, and he proceeded to get his contractor's license and set up shop.

Over the years we dealt with all types of business issues. And we could tell you countless stories about having to deal with employees, cash flow struggles and much more. Some things worked. Some things didn't. We paid a high cost for some of the lessons we learned. Yet through it all, I am glad we made this decision. The road is challenging, but worth it.

Our second corporation was in the bookkeeping and tax field. After working with a wide variety of businesses, I found common challenges that most business owners face. Business owners sell their widgets or services well; but because there are so many things to attend to, they just "wing it." The thing is, "winging it" produces "winging it" sales and "winging it" profits. Consequently, they are "flying by the seat of their pants."

Over the years I have been comparing flying an airplane to running a business. To me, there are many truths, analogies and similarities one can learn in doing so. This creative insight can provide clarity to owners and managers that can inspire them to a higher level of management.

Because business owners are terribly busy, I intentionally broke up the chapters into small "legs." These shorter chapters will allow you to enjoy the flying analogy, relate it to your own business and draw practical ideas of what you can do today to better your company.

At the back of the book, I have included four items. The first is a list of suggested readings. These are books I have read that I feel have good content to help you expand your business knowledge. Second is a glossary of accounting terms, in easy-to-understand language, to help you, as a business owner. The third item is a checklist that I created for reviewing financial statements, to help you confirm their accuracy and readiness for tax preparation. And the last item is a collection of favorite quotes to encourage you in your business.

At the end of each chapter is an icon showing a fist full of money. This is to challenge you to be proactive in taking your business to a new altitude. If you spend a few minutes answering the questions or doing the activity, I know you will find it helpful in making good management changes in your business.

This book has been written to provide the business owner with insight, practical solutions and encouragement. As you read, you will see that I have a strong desire to motivate the reader to be a better manager of all income, expenses, assets and liabilities.

Enjoy your flight,

Renee

Chapter 1
The CEO & the Captain

There are old pilots and there are bold pilots,
but there are no old, bold pilots.

Many small business owners are "flying by the seat of their pants." They wake up early, work hard to put food on the table and are exhausted at the end of the day, hoping they were productive enough to have two nickels to rub together in their pocket. Am I right?

What does it mean to "fly by the seat of your pants"? Most people know this saying to mean someone is deciding on a plan as they go along. It could also mean that a person is reacting to situation rather than being proactive and planning ahead. "Winging it" could be another way to say it. This saying actually emerged in the late 1930s in reports of a flight from New York to Ireland by Douglas "Wrong Way" Corrigan. Mr. Corrigan was a sound and accomplished pilot. He even worked on a special aircraft for Charles Lindbergh and was inspired by Lindbergh's transatlantic flight in 1927. He requested permission from the government to make a non-stop flight to Ireland, but his application was denied. In 1938 Corrigan told authorities he was going to fly to California, but he ended up in Dublin after a 29-hour flight. His airplane took off in the thick fog and airport officials said he had to first head east to avoid buildings before he could turn around and head west to California. Corrigan reported visibility so poor that he had to fly by his compass, and he swore he was headed west, although he was really headed east. Most people really believe that Mr. Corrigan wanted to bypass the officials and accomplish his dream of a transatlantic flight.

As a business owner, you are the CEO, the chief executive officer. The encyclopedia defines this role as the highest ranking officer or administrator in charge of the total management of the company. A CEO is usually the chairman of the board of directors, and typically the CEO has other officers beneath him.

Some of the responsibilities of a CEO are:

- ✓ To advise the board of directors
- ✓ To motivate employees in products, programs and operations
- ✓ To look to the future for change opportunities
- ✓ To formulate policies and planning
- ✓ To promote the organization's mission
- ✓ To manage human resources
- ✓ To recommend a yearly budget for board approval
- ✓ To manage financial resources

Most small business owners have many responsibilities. They are the President, Treasurer and Secretary of their own company, in addition to being the CEO. When you are in business, you need to take your business seriously so that you *act* like the CEO, whether you have 20 employees, 10 employees or none.

There is a saying in the aviation world: "There are old pilots and there are bold pilots, but there are no old, bold pilots." What does this mean? It means that pilots who are overly bold and take chances, will not survive long enough to become old. Pilots need to be cautious. Flying is a serious activity, especially when there are passengers involved. Pilots need to pay attention to the aircraft and the conditions in the environment. So too must all business owners pay attention to their business and the conditions that surround it.

CEOs are similar to the Captain of an airplane in seven ways:

1. They must be decision makers.

2. They must show leadership.

3. They must be constant learners.

4. They must be constantly alert to reduce the possibility of errors.

5. They must follow policies and procedures.

6. They must be on the offense.

7. They must be good time managers.

Let's explore how they are similar in the following chapters.

Challenge:

1. If you were to score how well your business is doing, overall, from 1 to 10, (1 = poorly, and 10 = extremely well), how would you rate it?

2. What is one thing you could do to improve that number?

3. Rank yourself against these seven qualities of a CEO, in order of your strongest (1) to your weakest (7):

   Good Decision Maker   _____
   Strong Leader   _____
   Constant Learner   _____
   Problem Solver   _____
   Policy Developer   _____
   Strong Warrior   _____
   Good Time Manager   _____

4. Right at this moment, are you flying by the seat of your pants?

5. Write out your purpose; that is, why you are in business.

Chapter 2
Authority Figure & Decision Maker

Believe deep down in your heart
that you're destined to do great things.

—Joe Paterno

The Captain has ultimate authority. He decides when it is safe to takeoff, and whether the course needs to be changed. It is his job to get passengers to their destination safely. With that goal in mind, he needs to make countless decisions during the flight.

The Captain knows there is a storm ahead. He decides to deviate from his preplanned course and go around the storm. In order to do so, he will need more fuel for the longer flight. If the Captain orders additional fuel for the aircraft, the dispatcher provides it. The Captain is not questioned.

If Air Traffic Control gives clearance for the pilot to takeoff, the Captain can refuse to do so if he does not feel comfortable with the conditions of the aircraft or the weather. He has authority not only over the airplane, but also over Air Traffic Control.

A great example of this is when Captain Larry Carr, an experienced pilot with American Airlines, was "cleared to takeoff" in Oklahoma City headed to Dallas in August 2007. The control tower reported "moderate to severe precipitation six miles south of the runway moving rapidly northward." The recommendation was to take an immediate right or left turn after takeoff. In recalling a similar situation in the past, Captain Carr decided to wait for the storm to pass. Less than one minute later, the control tower alerted him that there was a microburst at the end of his departure runway with a fifty-knot loss of airspeed. Bottom line: If he had attempted to takeoff, the airplane would have encountered the microburst at just the time of liftoff, lost airspeed and possibly crashed.

Captain Carr says, "If the pilot screws up, the pilot dies. If the air traffic controller screws up, the pilot dies. The Captain is ultimately responsible for the safety and operation of the aircraft and must question everything."

When a pilot is taking off, there is a forward speed or velocity called V_1. At this benchmark the pilot needs to make the decision to continue the takeoff or safely stop the airplane. When a pilot makes the critical decision to takeoff, it is one he, the crew and the passengers live or die by. Business owners do not usually make split-second decisions that could result in death, but they do make decisions that will affect the life and growth of the company. Also, the frequency of their decisions can affect a business. For example, if you tolerate unprofessionalism from your employees for 2 months, it will impact your company. But, if you tolerate unprofessionalism from your employees for 6 months, it will impact moral, productivity and possibly profits on a larger scale, the longer you take to make the adjustment. So the lack of decisions or the rate at which they occur will affect the business.

Let me tell you a story of two CEOs who handled their authority differently:

I recently met a business owner who'd had an employee for 15 years. The employee undermined the owner and was very disrespectful. When I asked her why she kept him, she said she was fearful of the impact on her business if she fired him. I was concerned with the impact that her company is seeing by keeping him. And sadly, the owner's health was being affected due to the stress. She did not have control of her own company and did not demonstrate authority.

I know another business owner who found that his employee was spending business time and using company computers to send excessive personal emails. When the employee was confronted, the employer reminded the employee of the employee handbook where this activity was not allowed. The employee was suspended for 1 day and the employee expressed respect to the employer. There were no other incidents.

Just as the Captain has full and final authority over the air-craft, so should the business owner have full and final authority over the business. With that view, the CEO will make decisions for the benefit of the business. The sad part is that most business owners are so wrapped up in the busy-ness of running the business, they do not take the time to look at their business and make needed decisions.

The Captain gets support from his First Officer, dispatcher, flight attendants and maintenance crews. He makes decisions based upon the reports he gets from the people around him. Similarly, a business owner needs to gather information from his team as well. Business owners cannot do it alone. Team members might include an assistant, attorney, CPA, business coach and/or marketing manager, to name a few. These advisors help and advise the CEO. However, it is ultimately the business owner who must make decisions for the company, just as the Captain does for each flight.

Challenge:

1. What decision have you been putting off that is affecting your business growth?

2. What have you been tolerating in your business that needs to change?

Chapter 3
The Leader

Leaders are made, they are not born. They are made by hard effort, which is the price that all of us must pay to achieve any goal that is worthwhile.

—Vince Lombardi

A Captain makes sure that his crew respects him so that when he gives an order, they follow. Captain Larry Carr likes to remind the crew, in a light and fun way, that he is the Captain. Before each flight, he briefs the crew, always starting with "I am the Captain, and don't let me forget it." It is important to be a leader the team can relate to. The air crew is a team and they need to look out for each other. It is a give-and-take relationship: The crew communicates with the Captain, and the Captain communicates with the crew.

A CEO can make decisions for the business, but will his staff follow him? Leadership and management style are important qualities that CEOs must address.

Business owners must possess strong qualities. They must be professional and knowledgeable, have integrity, be good communicators and be a pleasure to work with. Employees fail when their boss is indecisive, lacks communication skills and does not provide direction. Think about it: Would you rather fly with a Captain who barks out orders and is unapproachable, or a Captain who is knowledgeable and friendly?

Even if you just started your business, you can lead with integrity. How? Find someone to model yourself after, or model your company after another respected firm. You will be pleasantly surprised to learn that people are honored to share their experiences with you. Learn to think like the person possessing the skills you desire. Emulate that person. Read a book on leadership or listen to an audio book. Many good books are available; look in the back of this book for recommendations.

I see CEOs struggle by being too timid with their employees. CEOs cannot treat their employees like friends. It does not work. Do you tolerate your employees' coming in late frequently? Do you tolerate long lunches or personal use of the computer? This is stealing! Some business owners are so fearful that they allow their employees to dictate when they come and go and what they will or will not do. I see managers afraid of saying anything to their employees, because they do not want to rock the boat or feel they cannot maintain the business without that person. You will find peace of mind when you fire an employee who is falling short of expectations, undermining authority or stealing from you by being unproductive on the job.

A client of mine said her mistake in business was that she treated her employees like partners. They had a say in everything. By allowing this, the employees made decisions without considering the culture that the CEO wanted to create. Ultimately, the company folded because the employees undermined her leadership.

Yet a person does not want to be a business owner who is extremely stern with employees either. This creates an intimidating atmosphere in which employees become apathetic. This type of business owner has lost his passion, which makes the environment unbearable.

Avoid being so rigid that you do not consider input from your employees. It is wise to include their ideas; CEOs do not have all the answers. One person's IQ is less than the IQ of a group. Listening to the people who have their hands on the work daily is valuable. In fact, by your hearing their creative ideas, the company could save thousands of dollars.

So how does the business owner find the right balance? Do you want to be liked or respected? For me, the balance has been found through experience, practice, prayer, counsel from those who have gone down that path and a willing attitude to keep learning how to be a better leader.

Challenge:

1. Name a person or a company you can model your leadership style after.

2. Rate your leadership in the following categories from 1 to 5 (1 = poor; 2 = fair; 3 = average; 4 = above average; 5 = expert):

   Knowledge: _____

   Communication: _____

   Integrity: _____

3. Are you too timid or too stern?

Chapter 4
The Constant Learner

Formal education will make you a living;
self-education will make you a fortune.

—Jim Rohn

To earn your private pilot's license, you need 40 hours of flight experience. For a commercial license, you need 250 hours. An airline transport pilot license requires 1,500 hours of flight experience. How much experience is required of a business owner to create a business? For most industries, the requirement is to pay for a business license in your city. Anyone can be in business.

In preparation for each flight, the Captain and the First Officer are required to report to the airport at least one hour prior to the departure. They are required to review all information pertinent to that particular flight. Almost all of the information is included with the printed flight plan. This information always includes the planned route, altitude, planned fuel requirements, weather information at the departure airport, en route and destination airport. The report also contains the latest Notices To Airmen (NOTAMS) which cover any aviation hazards, airport information, en route information, and airport equipment outages. The entire package is usually 10-15 typed pages long. At the aircraft, the Captain briefs the crew, reviews the aircraft maintenance logbook, ground checks all aircraft systems and begins a series of written checklists.

Before each flight, the Captain prepares and reviews all information. How much reviewing does a business owner do before they step into the "cockpit" each day?

An airline transport pilot is required to have a medical exam by an FAA-certified Aviation Medical Examiner every 6 months. He also is required to undergo recurring training, involving several days of ground-school review and flight-simulator training. The frequency of the training depends on the individual airline requirements; it could be every 9 months or annually. The training and exams are a requirement by the FAA in order to maintain his flight qualifications.

Many business industries—insurance, securities, tax preparers, truck drivers, health care professionals, and others—have requirements for continued education. However, many business owners can operate for years without having to take a test or a class. This is dangerous not only for customers or clients, but for the life of the business. Then, you may ask, why do some people run their business without being professional and diligent?

One of the common mistakes I see business owners make is an unwillingness to "be a student." You need to be not only a student of your industry but also a student of business.

What is the latest trend for your industry? Does your competitor have the new and improved product or service? Know the pros and cons of all your products or services so you can recommend the best solution for your customers and clients. Are you unsure of what is out there because you have been looking down at the plow? Find a class that teaches the latest techniques in your industry, or read a book or join a club that discusses the topics that pertain to your business. Businesses fail because they lack innovation—the willingness to stay sharp. Knowledge is a powerful tool.

To me, successful CEOs are willing to learn and grow. Those who are not open usually do the same thing over and over, and their business either dies or stagnates. Just as the Captain receives flight training, so must the CEO receive continual training to improve the business.

There are so many things to learn; so many ways to improve your business. Hire a business coach to educate you in different aspects of business. Learn how to run a successful marketing campaign. Investigate how to earn passive income.

Challenge:

1. What can you do in the next 30 days to educate yourself to improve your business?

2. Write down three books (or audio books) you are interested in reading. Buy one of them this week.

3. Consider hiring a business coach or other professional to help you with an aspect of your business—marketing, bookkeeping, human resources, product/service profitability, legal, website development, tax strategies, etc. Write down one of these areas in which your business could most benefit:

Chapter 5
Errors & Omissions

*Anyone who has never made a mistake
has never tried anything new.*

—Albert Einstein

Pilot error is the cause of most airplane crashes. Pilot error can be described as a mistake, oversight, lapse in judgment or failure to exercise due diligence. Flying an airplane requires the Captain to be serious about his duties. No one person is perfect; it is unreasonable to expect perfection. Yet why is it seemingly okay for a business person to "wing it" when running a business? Time after time I see people so busy that they do not exercise diligence or good judgment. They think they will be able to deal with it all later. If this describes you, I implore you to get up, wash your face and commit to do whatever it takes to avoid CEO error.

Most pilot errors are the result of being distracted. Small errors can happen because of misinterpretation. A pilot can lose his license by making several flight violations due to errors. If there is a small mechanical problem, a pilot can become distracted and then make a bigger mistake.

Business owners deal with a lot of distractions too. Because of these distractions, they make errors. Owners who wear many hats in a company are so focused on making the sale and providing the product or service that they struggle with managing their company. This is when such owners spend their time working *in* their business, not *on* their business. With these distractions come missed opportunities and errors.

So do business owners receive violations in business like the pilot can? In my opinion, yes. They reap the consequences of not paying employer taxes, in the form of penalties and interest fees on taxes owed, and litigation for neglecting to uphold corporate standards.

When a business or employee makes a mistake with a client, the best thing to do is acknowledge the error, be humble and do your best to make it right. If you are a contractor and the work was not the quality it needed to be, then the work needs to be redone. If you are a service-based company and paperwork was supposed to be sent out in a timely manner and was not, then maybe a discount is given and the time it takes to fix the situation is not charged to the client.

If you expect perfection, you will be disappointed. However, clear communication and attitude are important. Let me give you an example.

A business owner was on contract with his customer. The contract stated dimensions for the product for a specific price. Realizing that a sizing error had been made, the business owner informed the customer of the error. The owner felt that since he made the error, he would stand by his price, even though the mistake would cost the company $1,500. Out of appreciation for the integrity, humility and attitude the business owner had displayed, the customer paid the corrected price for the size product received.

In July 1999, John Kennedy, Jr., his wife and sister-in-law were killed in an aircraft he was piloting. They were headed to Martha's Vineyard, where the family has a vacation home. John Jr. had 310 hours of flight experience, which included 45 hours of night flying. The FAA requires 250 hours to qualify for a commercial pilot's license. The National Transportation Safety Board investigation found no evidence of mechanical malfunction and determined that the probable cause was "the pilot's failure to maintain control of the aircraft during a descent over water at night, which was a result of spatial disorientation."

Spatial disorientation can be very serious. Steve Nation, a private pilot, told me a story of another pilot who was flying over water. The lights reflecting off the water gave the illusion that they were stars, so this pilot thought down was up and up was down.

Are you feeling that up is down? You are not alone. But, what can you do to change this? More answers lie in the following chapters.

Challenge:

1. How much of your day are you distracted and unproductive?

2. Are you frustrated with the number of mistakes you or your staff make?

3. When a mistake happens, how is your communication and attitude?

4. Figure out why or how a mistake occurred and write out a policy of how to handle the same situation in the future.

5. Are you disoriented and feeling upside down? Take a day off away from the office to figure out how to turn your company right-side up again.

Chapter 6
Policies & Procedures

Do or do not. There is no try.

—Yoda

Very few aircraft emergencies require immediate action. The first human instinct is to attempt to gain control of the aircraft. You have a much better chance of surviving if you take a step back, analyze the situation, gather all the data and follow your checklist. Every pilot has an operating manual that provides a checklist in case of emergency or abnormality. Whether it is an engine failure, fire or merely a tripped circuit breaker, there is a written procedure to follow. Captain Carr explains that "aircraft operating manuals have been written in blood." A seemingly simple minor problem can be compounded into a major problem if the time-tested written procedures are not followed.

In the real airline world there is no such term as "The Pilot." All airline cockpit crews are made up of at least two fully qualified pilots. The Captain sits in the left seat and the First Officer sits to his right. Each pilot has a full set of controls, enabling the aircraft to be flown from either seat. It is common practice for the Captain and the First Officer to alternate flying from the takeoff thru the landing on every other leg. The Captain always maintains the ultimate authority and responsibility for safe operation of the flight. You can think of the First Officer position as the "Captain in Training." Because major airlines each have thousands of pilots and flight schedules that are constantly changing, Captains and First Officers are rarely paired together for more than a month at a time. As a result of this constant re-pairing of pilots, aircraft operating procedures must be standardized to keep everyone "on the same page."

Airlines all have standard Aircraft Operating Manuals for each aircraft that they operate. These operating manuals have set procedures for all phases of flight, covering all possible situations from normal to abnormal to emergencies. For each set of procedures there is also a checklist. These separate checklists cover every phase of flight, beginning with the aircraft preflight, engine starting, taxi, takeoff, climb, cruise, descent, approach, landing and finally end, when the aircraft is parked back at the gate with the completion of the parking checklist. There is a checklist for everything. Nothing is left to chance. The more critical checklists, such as the takeoff checklist and landing checklist, are conducted in a verbal challenge-and-response method. For example, here is what happens when accomplishing the landing checklist. The Captain lowers the landing gear. The First Officer reads aloud, "Landing gear." Both pilots visually check for three green lights, and then the Captain responds, "Down and locked."

As you can see, the procedures for the pilots are very strict. Some would say they are extreme when comparing it to running a business. Yet, so many business owners are the opposite extreme where there are no procedures at all. They are making things up as they go. They are flying by the seat of their pants. The business owner must have policies and procedures in order for the business to run efficiently.

Think of it this way: How would you get your company to be a franchise, an entity where anyone can pick up the manual and follow the set procedures? When a manual is available, it saves time, prevents grief to all and ensures the consistency of the business. Just think about McDonald's. Do they change any part of the business depending on employee style, preference or emotion? No. Franchises allow ordinary people to be able to duplicate a system to do extraordinary things.

While it is so important to have your procedures written out, it is also important to give a guideline of creativity to employees. Let me give you two examples. Disney must have procedures documented in order to run their business. However, the employees (cast members) are told they can make decisions to ensure the happiness of the guests (customers). Also, I heard a story of a customer wanting to purchase a specific product from a company. The company was all out. The employee went out of her way to purchase it from their competitor and had it ready for the customer on the delivery date. Do you think that these examples generated customer loyalty? Absolutely!

Set procedures are important when it comes to paying employees. I would suggest having a written policy of tiered levels of pay. Having a policy helps in two ways: confidentially and productivity. First, I have seen so many businesses struggle with keeping payroll confidential from all employees. They are fearful that if they find out how much "Joe" is being paid, there would be a riot. Think of how your company would work if you had specific job duties that went along with specific rate of pay. Not only would you not have to worry if the employees are comparing wages, but then they would have a clear understanding of how to increase their level of competence in order to increase their level of pay.

Along with having a policy about paying employees, it is also important to have a written job description for each position in your company. The written list of job duties shows what you expect. Make sure you are detailed when listing what is required: List frequency, times and locations.

A client recently asked me how their company should handle an upcoming holiday with regards to paying their employees. I asked the owner, "What does your employee handbook say?" The owner said they do not yet have one in place.

If you have employees, then having an employee handbook is an important part of your business. This handbook describes the employer's expectations of the employee while outlining all the employee benefits. Having this written will summarize the policies and procedures to reduce any misunderstandings.

Employee retention is never 100%. Therefore, business owners need to instill and teach those who represent the business its culture and values. We do this by documenting what needs to be done in every situation. If you sell products, what is your return policy? Is it a full refund if the customer is nice, or is there a restocking fee for all returns? Everything needs to be documented in order to provide consistency, save time and prevent misunderstandings.

Challenge:

1. Do you have a manual that describes your business policies and procedures? If not, write down 5 regular business activities that you need to document:

2. If you do have a manual, skim it over to make sure it is current and complete.

3. Do you have an employee handbook? If so, is it up to date?

4. Do all the positions in your company have a written job description?

Chapter 7
The Warrior

Never let the fear of striking out get in your way.

—Babe Ruth

Following the events of September 11, 2001, the airlines and the FAA have made new policies to ensure the safety of passengers and crew. Because of the importance to bring passengers safely back home to their families, the United States government created an entirely new department called the "Department of Homeland Security." One part of this system is the Federal Air Marshall Service and the Federal Flight Deck Officer Program. Thousands of airline pilots have volunteered their own time and expense to be trained, sworn and deputized as federal law enforcement officers. The purpose is to provide pilots with a method of deadly force to prevent terrorist from taking over the cockpit. These qualified pilots carry firearms and are trained and ready to use them if an extreme case arises.

From a business point of view, we must have the mentality that business is war. Sun Tzu, a Chinese military strategist, is well known for explaining how in war you must have a plan. Your best defense is a well-thought-out offense. He wrote, "And therefore the general who understands war is the controller of his people's fate and the guarantor of the security of the nation."

The General in charge of the war, the Captain of an aircraft and the CEO of a business are controllers, respectively, of the fate of the nation, the passengers and the business. They must guard the safety of the people. Military writers have said that an important leadership quality is concern for the people.

So as the airlines plan to protect the passengers, so must the CEO plan to protect the integrity of the business. Too many business owners are reactive. That is, they react only to what happens around them. They do not take business seriously enough to be proactive.

Another way a business owner can protect his business is to incorporate his business. While I do not advocate that *all* businesses become corporations, there are appropriate times when a sole proprietor should incorporate. The first benefit is that a corporation will no longer pay self-employment taxes. The second benefit, in my opinion, would be for corporate liability protection. While there are good liability benefits from having an S-Corp or a C-Corp, there are also responsibilities.

If you own or manage a corporation, one of the benefits is the liability shield of protection. However, if you do not adhere to the rules and regulations, the protection that you thought you had can be penetrated and you could be vulnerable. Know what it takes to protect yourself from lawsuits. Anyone can sue a corporation and attack your corporate veil.

Here are three of the most common ways a corporation can loose its liability shield:

✓ First, commingling personal and business funds is a major wrongdoing. Do not pay your mortgage out of your business bank account and call it a draw or distribution. If you are serious about your business, you will keep business transactions separated from your personal activities. Keeping personal and business transactions separate not only helps with maintaining a clean corporation, but also shows credibility to the IRS in case of an audit.

✓ Second, if a shareholder has lent the corporation money, there must be documentation of the repayment plan, and interest must be charged. Draft a promissory note showing the amount of the loan, interest to be charged and the date and amount of payments.

✓ Third, annual minutes are required by each state. Several attorneys have told me that when a client hires them to file a lawsuit against a corporation, the first thing that they do is request the corporate minutes so they can pierce the corporate veil. Many business owners do not know how to put together the two documents—meeting of shareholders and meeting of directors. Protect your corporation and seek counsel.

Rise up and strap on your armor so you are ready for the business battlefield!

Challenge:

1. Name a time when you were reactive instead of proactive. How did that work for you? Describe what you would have preferred to happen:

2. Do you have the confidence that your business has the appropriate business structure (sole proprietorship, partnership, LLC, S-corporation, or C-corporation)? If not, seek counsel.

3. Are you commingling personal transactions in your business bank account?

Chapter 8
The Time Manager

Perhaps the very best question that you can memorize and repeat, over and over, is, "what is the most valuable use of my time right now?"

—Brian Tracy

A good pilot is a master of his time. His flights must arrive and depart on time. Fighter pilots measure time by the narrow margin of seconds. These trained pilots fly past the speed of sound and typically make decisions at up to 20 miles per minute. Now a CEO must be a good time manager as well, although not to this extreme. If the company commits to providing a product or service at a specific date for a customer, then all planning needs to be done with the end in mind. Leaders who need to manage their day need to prioritize—decide what is important. This is challenging, due to the many distractions owners face. Yet who wants to do business with someone who cannot show up on time?

If you have a home business or if you find you are distracted easily at the office, you need to recognize what "steals" your time and keeps you from being productive. Surfing the Internet, reading endless email, receiving unscheduled phone calls, and reading junk mail are just a few activities that can keep you from staying on task.

One of the best time-management activities I implemented in my business was to block time during the week to do specific activities. For example, I do not take any appointments on Mondays. I use this day to pay bills, invoice clients, plan my week, catch up on emails, etc. This is my administrative day. On Tuesdays and Thursdays I go outside the office to meet with clients. On Wednesdays and Fridays I have phone appointments and inside appointments. By blocking time, I am able to be more productive, with fewer interruptions.

Delegating is another good idea. Do you realize that you can potentially earn more money in your business by doing what no one else can do and delegating tasks that others can do? If you spend 5 hours a week cleaning your house, you can work 1 hour and pay for a housekeeper. This will give you back 4 hours of your week. If you can hire a virtual assistant to schedule your appointments, you can work 1 hour a week to pay for the cost to have your VA spend hours on the phone. You can hire a college student to open your mail, assemble your bills and do filing. Delegating can eliminate stress as well as decrease the number of hours an owner works each week.

Owners need to prioritize tasks that are urgent and tasks that have a lower priority. However, if you are a procrastinator, many of your items on your list do not get touched. These are common reasons people procrastinate:

✓ Fear of failure—what if I do not have the skills?

✓ Perfectionism—what if I cannot get it done perfectly?

✓ Poor time management—if only I had more time in my day.

Avoidance of projects is not a good business principal to live by. When you are in business, you cannot afford to procrastinate, because procrastination sabotages your success.

How do you balance it all? Here are a few suggestions:

1. Make a plan every morning for your day.

2. Prioritize your tasks.

3. Delegate, delegate, delegate (where possible).

4. Avoid procrastination—get it done!

When you complete a task that has been on your to-do list way too long, remember the peace that it brings when you accomplish your goal. Let this motivate you!

Kevin McCarthy's book, *The On-Purpose Person*, changed my perspective on time management. In his book he tells a story of how, when a person has figured out his purpose in life, he then spends his time according to his purpose. Mr. McCarthy uses a light switch to symbolize that a person's time is spent either on purpose or off purpose. This picture can help you visualize if you are staying on task.

When you know your purpose, you can be more productive. It is easy to want to do everything, especially all the fun things. However, people who want to fulfill their purpose in life need to be able to say no to the activities that do not help accomplish their goal. Sometimes we agree to do something because it is a good cause or we feel pressured to say yes. While many wonderful projects exist that we can be a part of, good time managers need to learn how to politely say no to those that are not directly connected to their purpose.

CEOs needs to be masters of their time in order to be productive.

Challenge:

1. Document the number of times you arrive to an appointment on time this coming week and the number of times you arrive late:

    Arrived on time: _____

    Arrived late: _____

2. Write down 3 tasks you could potentially delegate:

    Pick one to delegate this week:

3. What is one thing you have been procrastinating to get done? Do it today!

Chapter 9
Financial Statements & the Instrument Panel

Without vision, the people perish.

—Proverbs 29:48

When flying in the dark or clouds, how does a pilot reach his destination? He relies on his instrument panel to navigate the aircraft when there are no visual cues. The same is true for business. How does a company know where it is going? By relying on financial statements to state where they are and where they are headed.

Financial statements are the CEO's instruments. Like a Captain reads the instruments on the aircraft to navigate, so must business owners read their "financial indicators" in order to know where they are. The owner must know the purpose of financial statements, how they work, and what they mean.

In my years of working with business owners, I have found that many do not look at a profit and loss statement. Maybe you do look at the statement, but do you know how to interpret the numbers? And on the balance sheet, do you know your net worth? If you sold all your assets, could you pay off all your debts? If you are a serious CEO, you must be able to read your instruments—your financial statements.

Can you imagine running a business and not knowing how to read a financial statement? Don't be embarrassed, ask. It is important to understand for the stability of the company. Once business owners and managers can read the financial statements, they can make intelligent decisions.

Owners have come to me from all industry types. Some owners have no system of recording their income or expenses. Other owners have used Excel or tried to use QuickBooks but have given up. Some other CEOs have financial statements, but they are pages long and fraught with scattered and unreliable numbers.

Fighter pilots have instruments that show situation awareness. But with so many instruments, lights, and buttons to oversee, it can be too much when a pilot is in a critical situation. Fighter pilots just need to know the status of the enemy, status of the aircraft, or status of their weapons. Their instruments have combined screens to keep things simpler for the pilot. So too can CEOs have information overload. I recommend when this happens that owners clean their desk and make a to-do list. A clean desk and a list of priorities can give peace of mind.

Following is a profit and loss statement that shows income and expenses. Skim it and see what you conclude about this business.

Your Financial Flight Plan
Profit & Loss
January through December 2009

	Jan - Dec 09
Ordinary Income/Expense	
Income	
Sales	220,172.54
Total Income	220,172.54
Expense	
Advertising and Promotion	6,889.01
Bank Service Charges	10,513.68
Continuing Education	1,700.77
Depreciation Expense	8,472.46
Dues and Subscriptions	1,200.00
Insurance Expense	2,433.56
Meals and Entertainment	1,701.65
Office Supplies	5,691.16
Payroll Expenses	43,412.38
Postage	94.00
Professional Fees	32,914.91
Rent Expense	32,000.00
Telephone Expense	2,239.24
Travel Expense	623.71
Total Expense	149,886.53
Net Ordinary Income	70,286.01
Net Income	**70,286.01**

How does this statement compare to your own profit-and-loss (income-and-expense) statement? Make sure your statement is one page or less. Anything more indicates unnecessary accounts. Make sure all bank and credit card accounts are reconciled, checking for transpositions, omissions and duplications. What you call a deduction will deem how it is taxed. Make sure your transactions are placed in the correct account/category.

Robert Kiyosaki, a well-known investor, entrepreneur and educator, consistently speaks on the importance of financial literacy. He says numbers on financial statements tell a story. He explains that most people can read, but the comprehension level is different for everyone. If you are struggling, you need to get back to basics—reading and understanding financial statements.

Challenge:

1. Print out your Profit and Loss Statement for the current year. Write down:

   Total Income: _____

   Total Expenses: _____

   Profit/Loss: _____

   In which category or categories are you overspending?

2. Are your financial statements reliable, accurate and up-to-date?

3. Rate your knowledge on understanding how to read financial statements (1 = poor; 2 = fair; 3 = average; 4 = above average; 5 = expert):

Chapter 10
The Altimeter

We are what we repeatedly do. Excellence, then,
is not an act, but a habit.

—Aristotle

In flying an airplane close to the
ground, the pilot can lose the "big
picture." In flying at higher altitudes, the pilot can lose track of the
details of the land. How can a CEO
fly at the right altitude? By reading,
understanding and studying the
financial statements. These documents tell management at
what level the company is "flying" at that exact moment.

When in the air, the Captain needs to know, at all times, the
altitude of the aircraft. This is important so that the aircraft
does not hit another airplane or the mountain ahead. Altitude awareness is especially imperative when descending
and taking off, with so many other airplanes coming and
going.

Did you know that when you are flying east, you must be at an odd altitude, like 31,000 feet? And when you are flying west, you must be flying at an even altitude, like 32,000 feet. The altimeter is important because it shows the Captain at what altitude he is flying at any given moment. If the pilot is off on the aircraft's altitude, the results can be tragic.

The same is true for the Captain of a business. Very few people have come to me with clean and accurate reports they can rely on. And yet, so many owners operate their business either without having any financial statements or without having reliable statements. And they wonder why they are overwhelmed, stressed and grumpy! When you know exactly where you are, then you can make a plan to fly at a new and smoother altitude. If you are "flying in the red," then you must develop a plan of action immediately. Yet, when "flying in the black," don't let the monetary resource give you a false sense of security. Attention in both cases is important.

So you are running your business and you are flying at an altitude of 37,000 feet. You are headed towards your destination, but the company is experiencing some bumps along the way. As a pilot, you know the ride will be smoother at 27,000 feet. As a business owner, you know that cutting your spending by $10,000 will decrease the stress you feel when paying bills. What do you do? Do you know how much you are spending each month for telephone, meals, gas and advertising?

What would happen if a pilot were flying 200 people across the state and none of the three altimeters were functioning properly? Would the airplane crash? Possibly. Would you have faith in the pilot to get you to your destination? Probably not. Why, then, would CEOs run their businesses without reliable financial statements? Foolishness is my only answer.

 Some good advice I suggest is to have another person review your financial statements. Hire an auditor just to double check for internal controls. Hire a CPA to review your financial position. Hire a QuickBooks ProAdvisor to confirm that you are using the software accurately and efficiently.

The pilot uses his instruments to determine the status of the aircraft to enhance the passengers' comfort. For example, passengers can be thrown back in their seats and drinks spilled if a pilot uses unreasonable bank angles or pitch changes. However, when the aircraft turns or climbs to higher altitudes, the pilot can fly the airplane so that the change is barely noticeable to the passengers. In business, CEOs need to analyze the rate of change as to what the customer can tolerate. An example of changes in business could be price increases, changes in product line or changes in staffing. To keep profitable, change needs to occur, but a plan must be in place so it will not be upsetting to the client or employees.

What is net worth? It is taking your assets (furniture, equipment, property), subtracting your liabilities (credit card debt, loans) and then knowing how much is left over. Hopefully you have something left over; otherwise, you are upside down! True wealth is not the "things" you spend your money on, but the leftover amount after you pay what you owe.

Figuring out your net worth is important if you want to know your current financial position. Net worth is a simple calculation. Ever hear of that old saying, "Numbers do not lie"? Well, you could be driving the latest car, living in the largest home and still have a low or negative net worth.

Here are ways to increase your net worth:

1. Do not overspend! Reduce or even eliminate unnecessary expenditures.

2. Save. The earlier you start, the more you will accumulate over time.

3. Manage your assets (retirement accounts, investments) to get the best rate of return.

These are easy to write and easy to say, but results are seen with consistency and determination.

Take a look at the following sample Balance Sheet. It shows cash and other assets as well as debts and equity. See what you can conclude about this fictitious business from this statement. Compare this statement to your own.

Your Financial Flight Plan
Balance Sheet
As of December 31, 2009

	Dec 31, 09
ASSETS	
Current Assets	
Checking/Savings	
Checking Account	17,705.09
Savings Account	5,939.32
Total Checking/Savings	23,644.41
Accounts Receivable	
Accounts Receivable	20,384.60
Total Accounts Receivable	20,384.60
Other Current Assets	
Undeposited Funds	4,956.57
Total Other Current Assets	4,956.57
Total Current Assets	48,985.58
Fixed Assets	
Accumulated Depreciation	-8,472.46
Furniture and Equipment	41,638.57
Total Fixed Assets	33,166.11
TOTAL ASSETS	**82,151.69**
LIABILITIES & EQUITY	
Liabilities	
Current Liabilities	
Credit Cards	
American Express	5,820.33
Total Credit Cards	5,820.33
Other Current Liabilities	
Payroll Liabilities	3,948.37
Sales Tax Payable	364.97
Total Other Current Liabilities	4,313.34
Total Current Liabilities	10,133.67
Long Term Liabilities	
SBA Loan	98,264.29
Total Long Term Liabilities	98,264.29
Total Liabilities	108,397.96
Equity	
Capital Stock	2,000.00
Retained Earnings	-98,532.28
Net Income	70,286.01
Total Equity	-26,246.27
TOTAL LIABILITIES & EQUITY	**82,151.69**

As the Captain of your company, you must know at what altitude your business is flying. Are you making a profit? Are you operating at a loss? If a loss, is it a $2,000 dollar loss or $20,000 dollar loss? This is my call to action for the reader. Some business owners must get their heads out of the sand, brush themselves off and deal with their business affairs in a professional manner. I have seen too many business owners swallowed up with the busy-ness of the day and not managing what is right in front of them. You always reap what you sow.

Challenge:

1. If you added up all your assets and paid off your liabilities, would there be any thing left over?
    (Assets—Liabilities = Money left over)

    Asset Total: _____

    Liability Total: _____

2. Look at your altimeter (financial statements); does it tell you how you are operating your business and whether you will hit the mountain ahead?

3. Have a professional review and give you advice on how to improve your financial statements so they are more accurate and reliable.

Chapter 11
Radar & Light Indicators

*You will not find a fever
if you never take a temperature.*

—Unknown

Another instrument important to a pilot is the weather radar display. Weather conditions are watched closely by pilots, especially when in the vicinity of thunderstorms. Harsh weather will determine if a pilot will deviate from his planned route. What's great about the radar screen is that light rain will be displayed as a green mass, moderate rain as a yellow mass and heavy rain and thunderstorms as a red mass. Flying through the green mass will only get you wet, but you will have a smooth ride. The yellow mass will be a very bumpy ride. Flying through the red mass can be catastrophic. Extreme turbulence, heavy rain and possibly hail have the potential to badly damage or destroy the aircraft. Experienced pilots will attempt to avoid the yellow mass to get a smoother ride and will always go around the red or thunderstorm areas. Inexperienced pilots may attempt to fly through the storm and either quickly gain needed experience or sadly be the object of a National Transportation

Safety Board (NTSB) accident investigation. Be a smart CEO. Go around the storm. Watch your radar display to deviate from a potential rough experience.

All airplanes have red warning lights and yellow caution lights. A yellow light could mean that the oil pressure is low and needs attention. Red means something is very wrong, like an engine or cargo fire. How does a business owner see warning lights? By knowing when the numbers on the financial statement change. They can fluctuate with minimal variance (yellow light), or they can jump up or down drastically (red light). The great thing about accurate and up-to-date financial statements is that the changes can be easily spotted.

Another component on the instrument panel is the set of three landing-gear lights, which indicate that the wheels are "down and locked." If you are running your business and only two of the green lights illuminate, what do you do? Do you know what to check? Can it be as easy as changing a bulb? Do you land anyway, assuming everything is okay? When you expect a number to be a certain amount and it is not, the CEO must ask questions and dig for details as to why "the light did not illuminate."

One way to make sure your financial statements are "down and locked" is by reconciling all bank and credit card accounts. My heart sinks when a business owner asks, "Is that important?" Why enter the data if you are not willing to reconcile? Recently, my client deposited $9,598.00 in his business checking account in the month of April. In the beginning of May, I reconciled his bank account and noticed that this large deposit did not show on the bank statement. The client asked the bank about it and found that the bank had put the deposit into someone else's account! Would that affect your cash flow? Of course!

Reconciling will also help locate any unauthorized transactions. For another client, I found three mysterious automatic deductions in which the client did not recognize the vendor name. In an Internet search, I found that this vendor had reports of fraudulent activities. While it is rare to find that the bank makes a mistake, the most common errors I find is transposed numbers, omissions and duplications. So the question is, do you reconcile all your accounts?

One of my favorite statements to use in helping business managers is the profit and loss by month statement. This report shows income and expenses by category for each month. When looking at this report, a business owner can see inconsistencies. These variances tell a story. They indicate changes in the business. One of my clients calls it the "trend report." With this statement, the manager can make quick adjustments in the business within the year, rather than after the year has ended. Take a look at the statement on the following page and print your own profit and loss by month:

Your Financial Flight Plan
Profit & Loss
January through March 2009

	Jan 09	Feb 09	Mar 09	TOTAL
Ordinary Income/Expense				
Income				
Sales	56,072.50	52,857.18	49,857.21	158,786.89
Total Income	56,072.50	52,857.18	49,857.21	158,786.89
Expense				
Advertising and Promotion	550.00	1,345.97	2,496.29	4,392.26
Bank Service Charges	2,836.45	1,974.49	1,845.70	6,656.64
Continuing Education	357.80	299.00	97.99	754.79
Dues and Subscriptions	300.00	300.00	300.00	900.00
Insurance Expense	608.39	608.39	608.39	1,825.17
Meals and Entertainment	141.80	491.38	385.35	1,018.53
Office Supplies	316.67	3,160.43	207.68	3,684.78
Payroll Expenses	11,236.20	11,098.37	8,494.58	30,829.15
Postage	47.00	0.00	47.00	94.00
Professional Fees	9,634.05	10,428.52	7,457.10	27,519.67
Rent Expense	8,000.00	8,000.00	8,000.00	24,000.00
Telephone Expense	519.79	579.28	642.90	1,741.97
Travel Expense	623.71	0.00	0.00	623.71
Total Expense	35,171.86	38,285.83	30,582.98	104,040.67
Net Ordinary Income	20,900.64	14,571.35	19,274.23	54,746.22
Net Income	20,900.64	14,571.35	19,274.23	54,746.22

Challenge:

1. Currently, are you operating your business with the "radar" showing green (not too bad), yellow (warning, something is not right) or red (emergency evaluation)? Take appropriate action.

2. Do your financial statements show any warning lights? Print out your statements and highlight the items you are concerned about.

3. Print out your profit and loss statement by month and look for trends or inconsistencies. Figure out the reason and make any necessary changes in your company.

4. Are all of your bank and credit card accounts reconciled up to last month?

Chapter 12
Airspeed Indicator & Artificial Horizon

*A business that makes nothing but money
is a poor business.*

—Henry Ford

He looked straight ahead, trying to relax, but the commotion in the back of the plane was irritating him. Plus Tim could not get comfortable in the chair. There just was not enough room for his long legs. His wife, Sue, reached in her bag and handed Tim a water bottle.

"How long is this flight?" Tim asked his wife. "About 3 hours," she said. "Did you bring that book you wanted to read?" "Yes," he said, "but I do not feel like reading right now."

The Captain of the aircraft made an announcement. "Folks, we should be taking off here shortly. We are expecting some turbulence due to the thunderstorms over Houston. I will be making some course adjustments along our route to avoid most of it. We are expecting a few bumps along the way. I will most likely be keeping the seat belt sign on for most of the trip."

Tim and Sue were flying from Houston to Chicago to visit their daughter and grandchildren. Tim hated to fly. He hated the sensation in the pit of his stomach when the plane took off. He hated the idea of flying and not being able to see where he was in the air because the plane was surrounded by clouds.

Have you ever been near an airport and watched a large commercial aircraft takeoff? I remember parking my car in the flight path of San Jose Airport just to watch the planes. I sat there amazed at how a metal bird could get all that weight up in the air. Then I wondered how a person could think of all the details needed in order for this to occur. Amazing!

The airspeed indicator is a gauge on the instrument panel that tells pilots how fast they are flying. This is especially important when taking off and landing. During takeoff, the commercial aircraft weighing up to 600,000 pounds must be going fast enough to generate lift-off for a safe climb. When landing, the pilot must watch the speed so that they are not traveling so fast that they float too far down the runway prior to touchdown. Conversely, the pilot must not fly so slowly that the aircraft loses the required lift and sets down short of the runway. The heavier the aircraft, the faster the pilot must fly.

The same is true for a company. A business must pay attention to the speed at which it is moving. A company can be moving too slow. Maybe this is where an owner has been in business for a long time doing the same thing over and over, and the business becomes stagnant. Or, if a company is moving too slow, its customers or clients may start complaining and become dissatisfied or restless.

I have seen businesses that move too fast. They make hasty decisions without doing the proper research. An example of this is when two people jump into forming a partnership without weighing all the costs. Sadly, I can think of a handful of partnerships that did not end well. Both parties had expectations that the other party did not fulfill.

Moving too fast is not always a bad thing. If you have an employee who is stealing, proper action needs to be taken right away. If a client calls with a concern, the company needs to respond quickly. Timely communication will allow resolution. No communication allows the other party to think the worst.

Again, a careful watch of the company's financial statements will confirm whether it is moving forward in a safe manner.

What does your attitude indicate? An attitude indicator, also known as an artificial horizon, is an instrument used to inform a pilot of the orientation of the aircraft relative to the earth and sky. It will show pitch (up and down) and bank (side to side). This instrument will show horizon lines representing the wings and the nose of the airplane. The attitude indicator is imperative, especially when the visual conditions are lacking or limited. The interesting phenomenon about flying is that, when an aircraft is banked to the right or left for an extended period, a person's inner ear, which controls equilibrium, will adjust and think it is level when in fact it is not. The pilot must have visual sight of the actual horizon or totally believe his attitude indicator. With no visual reference and disregarding the attitude indicator, the pilot may bank in the opposite direction and set up the infamous "graveyard spin." Pilots must always believe their flight instruments. Similarly, it is crucial that a business owner be able to rely on his financial statements. He may feel that things are level and good, when in fact they are not.

If business owners operate their business "in the dark," "in the clouds" or "through the thunderstorms," then the only way to survive and not hit the mountain is to rely on accurate instruments like the airspeed and attitude indicator. Just as a Captain must rely on instruments to see beyond the dark, the snow and the rain, so must owners rely on accurate financial instruments.

How can they do that? The profit and loss statement shows income and expenses. The balance sheet shows assets and liabilities. Together, these statements indicate whether the company is on course or if it will land in Ireland rather than California.

Challenge:

1. No matter the size of your company, check your speed. List one thing on which you have been procrastinating (moving too slow.) Name one thing that you have been doing without having weighed the cost (moving too fast).

2. If you want to have confidence in the reliability of your financial statements, go through the checklist at the end of the book. When you are finished making any changes based upon that list, print a second set of reports for comparison. Get excited—this will be a huge accomplishment!

Chapter 13
Cash Flow & Fuel for the Aircraft

Be sure you know the condition of your flocks,
and give careful attention to your herds.

—Proverbs 27:23

It's 8:30 in the morning and Captain Wray is talking to his First Officer. "With the storms ahead, I am going to not only take an alternate course, but also fly at a lower altitude so that there will not be as much turbulence. Call the dispatcher and let them know to give us more fuel. We will need it flying at lower altitudes."

Fuel to an aircraft is cash to a business. Fuel allows the airplane to travel from one location to another. The fuel indicator tells pilots how long they can stay in the air. Cash flow in the business does the same thing—it gets you where you want to end up and tells you, the business owner, how long you can keep your doors open.

For small business owners, cash flow is one of the top areas in which small business owners struggle. How do you get the cash into the business? How do you budget expenses and know you have the funds to cover them? These are questions I hear frequently.

There is no magical formula. It is quite simple actually:

	Total of Cash on Hand
+	Incoming Cash from Clients
–	Bills to Pay
	_____
=	Ending Cash on Hand

Yes, I know it is sometimes difficult to wrap your head around the idea of money coming in and going out simultaneously. But, also it can become an emotional struggle. You have a great service or widget that provides a solution for many people; but when you go to pay the bills, it is depressing because of the lack of funds in your account.

The following table shows a simple way to calculate the ebb and flow of money. Look at it step by step and plug in your own numbers.

Weekly Cash Flow Projection				
	1/1/2009	1/8/2009	1/15/2009	1/22/2009
Cash in Bank Account	$5,462	$1,663	$3,948	$4,355
Incoming Cash from Clients	+$5,924	+$6,253	+$4,979	+$4,245
Total Cash	$11,385	$7,916	$8,927	$8,600
Bills to Pay	−$9,723	−$3,968	−$4,572	−$2,187
Ending Cash Balance	$1,663	$3,948	$4,355	$6,413

If your business is seasonal, you know that income will fluctuate. If your company is paid by commissions rather than a set monthly income, it can be difficult to plan. Just as the Captain of a commercial airliner will order more fuel because the forecast shows strong headwinds, so must the business owner plan ahead for the winds of change in business. If the income varies in your company, planning and budgeting are increasingly important.

So has an airplane ever run out of fuel? The answer is yes! In December 1978, a United airplane traveling from Denver to Portland ran out of fuel and crash-landed in a residential area. There were 24 serious injuries and 10 deaths. And why did the airplane run out of fuel? Read this carefully: *Only two of the three landing gear indicator lights were lit.* The airplane continuously circled around the airport while the crew tried to figure out the problem. The crew was so distracted by this problem that they did not pay attention to their fuel level. And the amazing part is that the investigation concluded that there was no problem with the landing gear. The report indicated that the unlit indicator light bulb had burnt out. Warning to owners: Don't take your eyes off your bank account!

What about the opposite problem? Have you ever known a company that is doing well and does not watch their cash flow? I have. Spending tends to be out of control. The company will make purchases because there is cash in the bank account, not that they have budgeted or planned for the expense.

What happens is the abundance of cash can blind the business owner giving a false sense of security. The truth is that they are either making extravagant purchases that they would regret later or not projecting the amount of money they will owe for taxes on the profits earned. When this happens, the CEO is handed a tax bill they cannot afford to pay. And, consequently, this forces the owner to close their doors. Warning: pay attention when there is surplus of cash and do not be deceived.

Challenge:

1. What is your "business fuel gauge" indicating to you? Rate how your business is doing in managing your cash flow (1 = poor; 2 = fair; 3 = average; 4 = above average; 5 = expert):

2. Using the Weekly Cash Flow Projection table in this chapter as a model, plug in your own numbers.

3. In the last 3 months, how much have you paid in bounced-check fees, late-payment fees or overdraft fees?

4. How often do you check your bank balance each month?

5. Are you spending money on unnecessary expenses?

6. Calculate the oldest invoices. Name 3 clients who owe you money and are past due:

   Follow your company procedure on collecting from them.

Chapter 14
Cash Flow Solutions: Keeping Fuel in the Tank

Treasure every moment you have. Time is a coin you can spend only once. Waste your time and you have wasted your money.

—Scott Lawrence

The FAA requires every aircraft to have an extra 45 minutes of reserve fuel on each flight in case of emergency. Do you have cash in the bank to cover bills for the next 45 days, in case of emergency?

My recommendation to any company is to first know what your monthly expenses are. Then, from that, start building a savings account to cover one week and then one month's worth of expenses. Why? This allows the business owner or accounts payable manager to pay bills on time and plan ahead.

I am sure you have heard the saying, "A penny saved is a penny earned." Back in the "olden days," people had a savings account. Yet, most Americans are not saving for that rainy day like their grandparents did. Individuals are living paycheck to paycheck, and some businesses are accumulating debt increasingly.

Remember the power of compound interest! For example, a 21-year-old person who saves $1,000 a year for the first 8 years can earn more money than a 29-year-old person who saves $1,000 a year for 37 years, assuming 10% compound interest per year in both cases. Hard to believe? Just look at the following table. Who would you rather be?

Who Would You Rather Be: You or Me?

Age	Me Payment	Value	You Payment	Value
21	1,000	1100	0	0
22	1,000	2310	0	0
23	1,000	3641	0	0
24	1,000	5105	0	0
25	1,000	6716	0	0
26	1,000	8487	0	0
27	1,000	10,436	0	0
28	1,000	12,579	0	0
29	0	13,837	1,000	1100
30	0	15,221	1,000	2310
31	0	16,743	1,000	3641
32	0	18,417	1,000	5105
33	0	20,259	1,000	6716
34	0	22,284	1,000	8487
35	0	24,513	1,000	10,436
36	0	26,964	1,000	12,579
37	0	29,661	1,000	14,937
38	0	32,627	1,000	17,531
39	0	35,889	1,000	20,384
40	0	39,478	1,000	23,523
41	0	43,426	1,000	26,975
42	0	47,769	1,000	30,772
43	0	52,546	1,000	34,949
44	0	57,800	1,000	39,544
45	0	63,580	1,000	44,599
46	0	69,938	1,000	50,159
47	0	76,932	1,000	56,275
48	0	84,625	1,000	63,002
49	0	93,088	1,000	70,402
50	0	102,397	1,000	78,543
51	0	112,636	1,000	87,497
52	0	123,900	1,000	97,346
53	0	136,290	1,000	108,181
54	0	149,919	1,000	120,099
55	0	164,911	1,000	133,209
56	0	181,402	1,000	147,630
57	0	199,542	1,000	163,493
58	0	219,496	1,000	180,942
59	0	241,446	1,000	200,137
60	0	265,590	1,000	221,250
61	0	292,149	1,000	244,475
62	0	321,364	1,000	270,023
63	0	353,501	1,000	298,125
64	0	388,851	1,000	329,037
65	0	**427,736**	1,000	**363,041**

Total Investment **8,000** Total Investement **37,000**
*Investment based up 10% compound interest

A common struggle CEOs have is to be able to pay bills on time. They feel like they are juggling, straining to get clients to pay so they can mail out a bill that is past due. Here is a technique I have personally followed for years. I mark my calendar to pay bills once a week. Then each week, I cut the checks and get the bills ready for mailing. Where the stamp belongs, I write the due date of the bill. Then I clip all the bills that need to be mailed into three bundles for the upcoming 3 weeks. This reduces my bank account, showing the bill paid, yet the bill usually sits on my shelf for days or weeks before it is mailed. There is something psychological about the money's being already gone from the checking account. You can also pay bills online this way and schedule the payment. In following this system, you will find two things happening:

1. You build a reputation for paying your vendors on time. What a joy to hear a vendor thank you for not waiting the typical 30, 45 or even 60 days to pay their bill. They are worth their wage. If it is within your means to pay them, then do so.

2. By paying your bills on time, you increase your credit score. A good credit score is vital when you apply for a loan. Credit scores are even used when purchasing car insurance or when an employer is selecting a candidate for a job.

Pilot Steve Nation says, "Most flight instructors will tell their students that the only time you will have too much fuel in the airplane is when you are sitting on the runway on fire." While the lack of money to pay bills can be stressful, the abundance of money needs wise management. If you do not have a watchful eye in both situations, the results can be the same: devastation.

If you are still struggling with paying your bills on time, I have another suggestion, although some may say I will be stepping on toes. I say that I am speaking the truth and some of you need to hear it. May I be direct with you? Stop spending more than you earn!

In working over the years with all types of businesses, one common thing I have seen is companies' overextending themselves. Many business owners are running their business at a loss and have thousands of dollars in credit-card debt. If you are in this position, stop and read this chapter carefully.

I am not telling you something that I have not personally struggled with myself. I want to tell you there is hope and peace. Years ago, business debt consumed me and my husband. We were paying the minimum on our credit cards which snowballed and increased the amount we owed, due to high interest rates. Obviously, what we were doing was not working, so we sought help. Through hard work and discipline, the large debt was paid off miraculously. We no longer have credit-card debt. The journey is a great story. You too can be debt free if you choose.

Don't misunderstand me. I am not against your taking out an SBA loan or charging expenses to a credit card to start your business or bump your business to the next level. I am not against your taking out an equity line of credit for business purposes. But do not borrow money when you have not weighed all the options and costs. Again, a CEO needs to be slow to make borrowing decisions. Avoid making a hasty choice just to ease your stress level for the moment. Avoid flying by the seat of your pants!

Cash flow is the key to a healthy business. Any business owner will tell you that cash flow is a typical challenge. Your accounts receivable do not mean much until they hit your bank account. Here are some suggestions on managing your cash flow.

✓ **Manage your spending**—justify your expenses to be ordinary and necessary to run your business. Avoid extravagant purchases; reckless spending will cripple your business later.

✓ **Monitor your money**—regularly watch your bank accounts. This includes having a budget and monitoring where you are.

✓ **Collect payments quickly**—have a method in place to collect on delinquent accounts, to encourage timely payments.

✓ **Disburse money slowly**—watch when your bills are due and do not pay early unless there is a discount incentive.

✓ **Have a cash reserve in good times and lean times**—it is important to have a savings reserve to fall back on.

Income will also fluctuate with your strategies. If you decide to implement a marketing campaign (which every business should) to promote a specific product or service, your income will increase. If you want to get a better grasp on cash flow coming in, watch your key business indicators. On a daily, weekly and monthly basis, I watch the number of free consultations I provide to prospective clients that might result in more sales. I also track the number of service agreements I send out, because that will indicate increased revenue as well. Think of this report as your business cockpit panel. Being able to track your marketing methods and results can indicate upcoming cash flow.

Challenge:

1. How much money do you need per month to cover your expenses?

2. Build a cash reserve. How much do you spend each week?

   Increase your reserve for one month's expenses to help reduce the stress of paying bills. You will find peace of mind when you do.

3. How often do you pay bills each month?

4. Do you have marketing campaigns? From your marketing ideas, start to track calls and inquiries as a method to track cash flow. Create a chart that shows this activity that you or your employees can easily document.

Chapter 15
Budgeting Profits: Preventing Leaks

*Unless you try to do something beyond what
you have already mastered, you will never grow.*

—Ronald E. Osborn

What is the amount of your net profit? Do you know? If you show a loss, do you have a goal of the profit level you want to reach – 3% profit, 10% profit, 20% profit? Here is a formula and a different way I want you to think about profits. This new way of thinking will be immediately helpful to your cash-flow struggles. In March 2008, I heard Brett Harward, CEO of Manifest Management Services, speak about managing numbers in business. Here is the formula he told us: Income minus profits equals expenses! Think about it. Read it again.

Compare your budget to the example below. Factor in your profits as an "expense" item.

Average Business Budget

Expense Item	% of Expense
Advertising & Marketing	2
Auto Expenses	1
Bank Fees, Merchant, CC	2
Continued Education	0.5
Equipment	3
Insurance	2
Materials/Supplies/Misc.	25
Meals & Entertainment	0.5
Office Supplies	2
Officer Wages	7
Payroll - Employee	25
Postage	0.5
Professional Fees	2.5
PROFIT	**5**
Rent	5
Taxes	15
Telephone	1
Travel	1

Total Percentage of Expenses   100.0

Notes: (1) This budget is general in nature. Depending on the industry or the business, the amounts will vary.
(2) Contractors will have higher labor, material and auto expenses.
(3) Administrative companies will have higher expenses for office supplies.
(4) Retail stores will have higher merchant fees.

Study the general expense items and the percentages allotted above. I encourage you to create your own in Excel. Write out regular expenses in your business to figure out how much you should be spending in each category. You will discover it is not as easy as it looks to get to 100%. You will find that your percentage will exceed 100, and it will take some negotiation to get your budget to balance.

So if you want to earn 5% profits, you need to plan to spend only the remaining money on expenses. Usually this means a business must cut some of the unnecessary spending. I have seen many owners each year, scroll down to the bottom line of the financial statement hoping, praying for a profit. Are you kidding me? "Hoping and praying" for a profit? They should be *planning* for their profit, knowing exactly where they are throughout the year.

When you follow a budget, the company makes purchasing decisions without emotion. Don't look at your bank account to determine if you will hire an assistant or sales person, buy that asset or agree to an extensive marketing campaign. If you do, it will affect your profits. Without making adjustments in another area, it would be allowing money to leak out of the bottom of the bucket.

When you have a budget set up like the example in this chapter, it is important to watch your monthly financial statements to see if the percentage of expense varies. A slight variance up or down will affect your profits. Are you paying attention?

Cash flow can be depressing, challenging and stressful if you are flying by the seat of your pants. Every business must have a budget. Every business must have a savings. Every business must have a plan for profits, or there will be no profits. Don't struggle in this area any longer. Start today to do whatever it takes to find peace of mind.

Challenge:

1. Create a budget and factor-in a profit. What profit percentage are you aiming for? _____%

2. What expenses do you need to reduce in order to reach your profit goal?

3. Track your profits (or losses) monthly.

Chapter 16
Business Management & the GPS

If you don't know where you are going, you will probably end up somewhere else.

—Laurence J. Peter

A GPS—Global Positioning System—is a navigational system involving satellites and computers that can determine the latitude and longitude of the aircraft. Pilots used to rely on ground-based radio navigation aids. Now the GPS system is primarily used to navigate to the destination. It provides a large digital map indicating current location and destination. It also displays known terrain and other obstacles.

With the aid of a GPS, the Captain can anticipate obstacles in the flight path. A business owner must also. Just as the GPS shows a Captain the conditions of where the aircraft is headed, the CEO must be able to see the bigger picture of where the business is headed.

Knowing the terrain along the route of flight is of huge importance to a pilot. The GPS display is color coded. If the area is green, then the aircraft is clear of the mountain range below. Yellow means a potential threat, and red means immediate danger. Business owners need to have the business GPS turned on. Are you running your business in the green, yellow or red zone? Will you hit the top of Mt. Whitney because you have no clue how low you are flying? Are your eyes opened to see the colors on the GPS screen to know the conditions ahead of you?

Corporations have shareholders who elect a board of directors. This board elects the officers of the corporation to take care of the daily activities of the corporation. What would happen if all business owners had to report to a third party for every aspect of business? Think about this: If all business owners were required to write out their business plans, provide financial statements and budgets, and account for all business activities, I know there would be a rise in responsibility. There would be no room for complaints or excuses. There would be no room for laziness. Just as a Captain is accountable to explain what he did or did not do during a flight, so must business owners be comfortable explaining their actions to a third party.

Budgets are a huge part of management. Yet, I have found that most business owners have no idea what they are spending per month for overhead expenses. Looking over your profit and loss statement weekly or monthly at a minimum is a must. Reviewing the budget with your team of advisors is important. I have also found that reviewing expenses with key employees can invite insights as to how to reduce costs and become more efficient.

Having a clear mission statement can help business owners navigate or pinpoint their purpose. Knowing why you are doing something will motivate you. It will give you passion when times are difficult. It will provide you fulfillment and joy, knowing you are making a difference in the lives around you. A pilot has a mission: to take the passengers safely from one location to another. What is your business mission?

Pilot and businessman Gerald Kerr describes flying either by hours of boredom or seconds of terror. After a pilot takes off, there can be many hours of smooth flight, repetitively monitoring the aircraft. Yet, in an emergency, there can be seconds of sheer terror when something goes wrong. And, in business, in a quick blink, a CEO can be faced with a key employee's quitting, a vendor's discontinuing a product when sales have been soaring or a problem with a contract that becomes a pending lawsuit. This is where having procedures and a business plan in place will help reduce the business owner's panic level.

Before takeoff, a pilot will review the weather forecast, the radar, the charts and the winds; he plans. Owners and managers must also be planners. They need to review the financial statements, seek counsel and keep up on business trends so they can plan as the winds of change fluctuate up and down.

When you say to a travel agent, "I want to plan a trip," the first thing the agent asks is, "Where do you want to go?" So, where *do* you want to take your business? As a business owner, you must ask yourself this question frequently. Your business destination is important. Do you want to have a small business and work a minimal number of hours to bring in extra income to your personal budget? Or, do you want to grow your business with 20 employees and manage them as they do the work? Or maybe you want to manage them as you sip your favorite beverage on the wooded deck of a secluded home in the redwoods.

Think long term. A company is born, but what is your exit strategy: To sell your business? To have your key employees buy you out? To close the doors and walk away? All good owners must manage their business with the end in mind.

And why do 80% of businesses fail in the first 5 years of opening their doors? They fail because of three things: lack of time, lack of desire and lack of knowledge.

Time   Either the owners are running around spending 50, 60, or 70 hours a week in the business, or the owners are lazy and bury their head in the sand to avoid dealing with unpleasant situations.

Desire   owners have no desire to deal with taxes or reconciling. They would rather spend their time generating income and doing what they do best.

Knowledge   Leadership, management, record keeping; these are not the reasons people start a business. They did not get a degree in management; they only found a solution to a problem and wanted to share it with others. But to stay in business and thrive, owners must make a commitment not to wing it.

Three simple solutions: No time? Make the time. No desire? Delegate. No knowledge? Get educated.

I have learned that every business "flies" at one of four levels.

The first level is running a business at a loss. The first step to managing your business is to know the exact amount of your loss and track it consistently. When CEOs have this information, they can make decisions for improvement.

The second level is running a business at a breakeven point. This is where the income equals the expenses.

The third level is running a business and being able to set goals of specific profit margins, such as 3%, 5%, 10% or 20%.

The highest level of business is when a company is able to plan and take advantage of tax strategies such as deferring taxes by making needed asset purchases, medical plans, 401k plans, and many others.

When business owners can identify which level their business is in, they can press forward to reach the next level of success.

Challenge:

1. Does your business GPS tell you that you will hit the mountain or fly right over it?

2. Rate how well you are managing your business (1 = poor; 2 = fair; 3 = average; 4 = above average; 5 = expert):

3. Good business owners commit to managing the business. Write out a statement that shows your commitment:

4. Write out your mission statement that shows your personal or business purpose:

5. I challenge you to determine what stage your business is in (loss in business, breaking even, generating a profit, or creating tax strategies):

   Now find two things you can do to bump your business to the "next altitude."

6. If you had to report to a third party on all aspects of your business, what area would you be embarrassed to show?

Chapter 17
Planning Ahead

The general who wins a battle makes many calculations ... here the battle is fought. The general who loses a battle makes but few calculations beforehand. Thus do many calculations lead to victory and few to defeat.

—Sun Tzu

A pilot would tell you that in order to fly in a straight line you must make a tremendous number of corrections in order to reach your destination. Because of wind and other factors, the Captain is continuously checking and adjusting. Pilots are constantly "coarse correcting" due to the weather conditions. The same needs to be true for a CEO to manage the business. A business owner must be able to analyze the situation and make "course corrections" in order to reach the company's financial destination. Expect that adjustments will need to be made. Anticipate that you will need to pay attention so you can make changes in your business.

What worked last year may not work for this coming year. Things change: economy, technology, labor force and trends.

A good manager consistently evaluates situations and makes adjustments. A good manager anticipates change instead of just reacting to it.

An experienced pilot will avoid last-minute planning by estimating time of flight, fuel burn, and route in order to review the different scenarios. Every Captain has a plan for any conceivable "what if" scenario. Experienced pilots can anticipate problems before they arise. Serious business managers must also take the time to plan out important factors in business. I see so many business owners reacting to their environment because they are so busy working *in* the business. Are you managing or reacting?

As the CEO, you need to think through the process of steering your company. Think about how you want your company to function and what it will take to get it there. *Rod Machado's Instrument Pilot's Survival Manual* has a great quote: "The two most important things in aviation are the next two things. Develop your ability to think ahead of the airplane. A pilot's invincibility lies in the mental preparation for every flight." Every business owner, too, needs to be mentally prepared to do business each and every day. Mental awareness is essential to success.

Having a business plan helps business owners and the board of directors navigate the business more efficiently. A business plan may include:

1. *Business Description* – describes the industry, type of entity, officers/owners and their expertise and how the company provides a solution to its clients.

2. *The Market* – describes clients, potential clients, ideal clients, competition and what makes the company unique.

3. *Product & Operating Plan* – describes the products or services that will be sold, inventory plan and how products and services will be provided.

4. *Advertising* – describes the different ways of promoting the company's products or services.

5. *Risks* – describes the financial risks, marketing risks and strategies to minimize the risks.

6. *Objectives and Goals* – describes business goals for the first, third and fifth year of business, outlining gross sales, profits, budgets, salaries, loans, advertising and more.

7. *Financial Chart* – describes the projected income, expenses and profits over a 1-, 3- and 5-year timeline.

While it is important to create the best business plan possible, it is just as important to acknowledge contingency plans. Every commercial aircraft has to have a back-up system. For example, there are back-up hydraulics, electrical, pressurization, fire detection, flight instruments, engines and even two capable pilots in every large airplane. For an airliner to be certified, it must be capable of completing the takeoff, climb, flying and landing at its maximum weight after the total loss of power from one engine. If any system fails while flying, there is a back-up system. There has to be! So, every business needs to have a back-up plan because situations will always arise that will change the course of a business. It is good to have Plan B in writing, in case Plan A does not work out as projected.

Here is another example of how planning ahead can help a business: Southwest Airlines has been purchasing low fuel prices for years. Many reports say that Southwest would have been at a loss without the benefit of locking in the fuel savings years ago. With the rise in oil prices, this Dallas-based company was wise to purchase these contracts, since fuel and labor were the top expenses for their company. Not only was the company smart about purchasing the fuel when the prices were lower, but they had the money available to lock in the lower prices. Southwest has a track record of years of profits, while most legacy airlines no longer have the cash reserves they once had. And now, with the price of fuel drastically increasing, other airlines are operating at a loss.

The use of these fuel hedges has helped Southwest maintain its profits during the oil situation related to the Iraq War and Hurricane Katrina:

Year	Price hedged per barrel
2007	95% hedged at $50/barrel
2008	65% hedged at $49/barrel
2009	50% hedged at $51/barrel
2010	25% hedged at $63/barrel
2011	15% hedged at $64/barrel

While purchasing a hedge on energy prices is risky, Southwest has received much positive press for this business risk.

As business owners, we can look at this Southwest Airline example and glean some ideas. First, this business planned for the future. They looked ahead. They had a vision. Second, in establishing this vision, they set aside profits in order to have the options. These options allowed them to be successful in the coming years. Many of us will never be in the situation that Southwest was, but we can certainly use these examples on a smaller scale that relates to our own situation. What can your business do to plan for future expenditures? What can you do today to provide good tax advantages in the coming years? A good manager is thinking ahead, not just trying to get through the coming month.

Ever hear the saying, "Proper planning prevents poor performance"? My high school teacher, Mr. Bruce Allen, had this mantra, and it has stuck with me. So when is the best time to prepare for an audit? If you want to prevent poor performance, the best time is as you go along in business. Find out what needs to be done to be organized, in case the IRS pulls your number.

Then there is the other popular saying, "Those who fail to plan, plan to fail." It is true, unless you are super lucky. If you do not plan, you are flying by the seat of your pants. And, if you do not plan, your business is doomed to crash.

Another saying that might not be as well known is, "The difference between fraud and tax planning is timing." It is fraud if changes are made in the financial statements after the year has closed. However, if you know the condition of the business, then with planning, taxes can be projected and deferred to the following year.

My all time favorite saying is, "You cannot manage what you cannot measure." A person needs reliable data in order to make the best decisions. All CEOs need to be good managers, and they can do so by thinking and planning ahead.

Challenge:

1. Do you have a business plan written and updated within the last year?

2. Southwest Airlines thought ahead and planned. What can you do today to plan for the future of your business?

3. What do you need to do to "course correct" the route you are on?

4. Are you mentally prepared to plan ahead in your business? How can you better prepare?

5. If changes are occurring in the economy or industry trends, what do you need to do to anticipate your customer or business needs?

Chapter 18
Goal Setting

What you get by achieving your goals is not as important as what you become by achieving your goals.

—Zig Ziglar

Goals. Do you get excited when you hear that word, or do you cringe? Again, if you are serious about your business, then you will be serious about making a plan. A goal is not something you wish for or just a good idea. It is something you are hungry to accomplish. Every pilot has the route written down. Is your plan for your business written? You may not achieve all your written goals, and sometimes your goals will change. But I have heard that the importance is not in *reaching* all your goals. The important issue is that you *set* goals.

To make the plan more achievable, goals need to be:

1. Attainable – break them down into smaller, attainable milestones.

2. Time sensitive – set a date for completing each step in the plan.

3. Written – commitments stick better when you log them.

When you set a larger goal, figure out how long it will take to attain, and then plan backwards. If you plan to accomplish a project, financial goal or growth goal within the year, then it is easier to break down the goal into smaller increments.

Goals need to be revisited often. If you set a goal for achieving a specific income amount for the year, you need to confirm that you have reached the monthly goal. Airplane engines are required to be inspected frequently. Engines are looked at not just for failure, but for wear and tear. Goals, business plans and procedures also all need to be reviewed and updated regularly.

Yet, as you live out the journey of reaching your goals, the best thing is not only to attain the goal, but also to build character. So the saying goes, "Does a contractor build the house or does the house build the contractor?" As individuals we need to hunger for our character to be built through the journey of planning and achieving our goals.

I will never forget what our pastor, Kyle Windsor, shared with us about his list of goals. He has a personal list of things he wants to do before he dies. Taking his suggestion, I have made a list of things I want to accomplish in my life. One of the goals was to skydive. Another was to go on a police ride-along. I have checked both off my list. Another goal is to travel to Switzerland and Hawaii with my husband. I highly suggest that you make a list of things you want to accomplish. Then you can say you lived life without regret.

Goals can help you better your service, reach a new income level, target opportunities and growth and keep you focused. But why do many people not set goals? Perhaps they do not know how. Or, when they do set goals but do not attain them, they become discouraged.

For me, I keep a binder close by. I write down my "wish" list of things I want to accomplish not only in business, but personally. Ideas could be goals having to do with monthly income, marketing, increasing profits, new clients, increasing cash flow, or improving the accuracy of financial statements. Sometimes my list changes due to new additions or else deletions of things that I thought I wanted to target but no longer consider a priority. The fun part is putting that date in the margin of when the goal was accomplished.

Planning ahead, setting goals, writing out a business plan, and creating a budget are all ways business owners can be good managers of business assets. If CEOs do not plan where they want the business to go, the results will be left to chance. Many of the business owners I have known have poured tons of time, energy and heart into their business. Because of all that passion they possess, I urge business owners to take action, today, and navigate their business intentionally.

Challenge:

1. What character traits are you developing as a result of your business?

2. Write down three goals that you can set to attain in 1 month, 3 months, and then in 6 months.

3. Start a list of things you want to accomplish.

Conclusion

The main on the top of the
mountain didn't fall there.

—Unknown

Dream ... look to the future and make a plan. If you are flying in one direction and do not like the results, what can you do today to course-correct for your destination?

This is your call to action! This is where you stand up and say you have no regrets. We all have one opportunity—to live each moment. We need to live it to the fullest, whether in business or in our personal life. In the previous chapters, we have compared, in a fun and creative way, flying an airplane to running a business. Stories and practical tips have been shared. You have been provided questions to explore further. All of this is to motivate you to take your business seriously enough that you will be the best manager of it.

So, as a great manager, what can you do to prevent your company from "flying by the seat of its pants"?

1. **Be the CEO you were meant to be.** Demonstrate leadership and authority. Be a constant learner of your industry and of business. Set up policies and procedures to minimize errors and prepare for the business battlefield. Be a master of your time by prioritizing your day.

2. **Know where your company stands,** through accurate financial statements, so they can direct you to reach your destination.

3. **Take control of your cash flow** so your company can thrive!

4. **Choose to navigate/manage your assets and liabilities** as though you were accountable to someone else.

While the reason for writing this book has been to awaken you, the business owner, to the realities of business management, I also want to remind you of one other important detail. The balance of work and home can be challenging. In your pursuit of doing the right thing in your business, remember to take the time to love your children—for the young ones, tuck them in and kiss them goodnight; for the older ones, tell them how wonderful they are and how much you love them. Remember to respect and communicate with your spouse. Get away together to keep your bond strong. I feel it is true: Behind every successful person is a loving and encouraging spouse. I think that there is a strong correlation between a successful business owner and a home in which harmony resides. So, right now, commit to do whatever it takes to bring peace to your home so you can have peace of mind in the workplace.

Take another deep breath ... relax your entire body. Hold still now. Can you see it beyond the clouds? It's out there. You can be the CEO that you were meant to be. Your business can thrive. All you need to do is stand tall and step into the cockpit. Place your hands firmly on the wheel and manage the team around you. You can reach your goals. You have the skill and the passion. Get ready to takeoff and enjoy your flight as you experience freedom, peace and contentment.

Ladies and gentlemen, fasten your seat belts and enjoy your flight!

—Renee

Glossary of Accounting Terms

Above the Line
> a phrase used to describe income and deductible expenses

Account
> transactions that are determined to be the same and grouped under one category

Accounts Payable
> the amount a business owes to its vendors; bills and obligations a company must pay in the future

Accounts Receivable
> the amount a business earned but has not yet collected

Accrual Basis
> a record-keeping system in which income and expenses are recognized when clients are invoiced or bills are received, regardless of when they are deposited or paid

Adjusting Entry
> a journal entry for the purpose of correcting a ledger account or bringing it up to date

Amortization
> the gradual extinguishment of any amount over a period of time on a note or non-tangible asset

Assets
> cash, equipment, vehicles, land and/ or buildings that a company owns

Balance Sheet

> a statement of the financial condition of a business at a certain date, showing its assets, liabilities and capital investments

Below the Line

> a phrase used to describe non-deductible income and non-deductible expenses

Board of Directors

> persons elected by the stockholders to advise and assist management with the corporation's affairs

Breakeven Point

> the volume point at which revenues and costs are equal; no profit, no loss

C-Corporation

> a business that has shareholders and officers, pays taxes at the corporate level and files an 1120 tax return

Capital Stock

> money paid to the company by investors to own a piece of the company

Cash Basis

> a record-keeping method whereby entries of income are made when received and expenses are counted when paid

Chart of Accounts

> a systematic arrangement of the accounts for a business, generally listed according to assets, liabilities, equity, income and expenses

Cost of Goods Sold

> the purchase price of goods bought in order to assemble and resell for a profit

Debit

> a bookkeeping entry posting an increase to an asset or expense or a decrease to a liability or income

Depreciation

wear and tear of a fixed asset, which decreases its value; this number shows as a negative number on the balance sheet to decrease the value of the assets

Distribution

profit distribution to stockholders in an S-Corporation

Dividend

profit distribution to stockholders in a C-Corporation

Draw

profit distribution to a sole proprietor

Equity

any right or claim to assets in the business

Expense

ordinary cost that occurs when running a business

First In, First Out (FIFO)

a stocking system in which the inventory acquired earliest is assumed to be used first; the inventory acquired latest is assumed to be still on hand

Fiscal Year

a 12-month period that does not end on December 31

GAAP

generally accepted accounting principles

General Ledger

all the transactions summarized in all accounts

Goodwill

the gross value of a business beyond the book value

Income

money earned that increases the total of assets arising from sales

Inventory
> for a manufacturing firm, the sum of finished merchandise on hand, raw materials and material in process; for retailers and wholesalers, the stock of salable goods on hand

Journal Entry
> recording of a business transaction where the debit amount equals the credit amount

Liability
> an amount the business owes to a creditor; an example is a long term loan, notes payable, accounts payable or credit card

Last In, First Out (LIFO)
> a stocking system in which the inventory acquired latest is assumed to be used first, whereas the inventory acquired earliest is assumed to be still on hand; an inventory valuation method

Net Profit
> income minus expenses

Officer
> in a corporation, a position elected by the shareholders; president, secretary or treasurer

Owner's Equity
> the number on the balance sheet representing the difference between assets and liabilities

Partnership
> an arrangement whereby two or more people merge forces so that each will benefit, with profits and losses shared jointly; partnership files a 1065, and a K1 is issued to each of the partners to pass on the profits or losses to their personal return

Profit and Loss (P & L) Statement
> a financial statement that shows income minus expenses, resulting in a profit or loss

Retained Earnings

the combination of profits and losses over the period of years that the company has been in business

S-Corporation

a business that has shareholders and officers; this business does not pay taxes at the corporate level, but each shareholder receives a K1 that flows the profits or losses to each shareholder's personal tax return; the corporation files an 1120S

Sole Proprietorship

a business owned by one person, the sole proprietor; the business owner files a Schedule C tax return and declares the business profit or loss on the personal 1040 tax return

Stockholder

an owner of shares in a company

Undeposited Funds

an account that is used to simulate the cash drawer; this is the account that accumulates money before that money is deposited into a bank account

1099-Misc

an IRS form used by a company or individual to report payments to a vendor that has received, from that company or individual, over $600 in a calendar year for services

W-2

an employer-generated payroll form used for tax-reporting purposes

W-4

an IRS form that must be filled out by a newly hired employee; includes name, address, social security number and withholding amount

W-9

an IRS form that a vendor fills out to indicate the vendor's taxpayer identification number

Your Financial Flight Plan

Checklist for Clean Books

Here are some things to check to make sure your books are clean:

- ❑ All bank accounts are reconciled.

- ❑ All credit card accounts are reconciled.

- ❑ Check for any old, uncleared items in the bank and credit-card registers.

- ❑ Make sure there are no negative numbers on the financial statements. The only legitimate negative numbers would be depreciation, owner's equity and a refund.

- ❑ Make sure the chart of accounts is clean. Merge duplicate or similar categories. Make sure there are no "other" expenses, for example "Advertising—Other." Make sure the chart of accounts is in alphabetical order.

- ❑ Make sure there are no uncategorized expenses.

- ❑ Make sure the credit card charges are entered through the end of December. With the cutoff date of credit cards, sometimes you must wait for the statement in February to get transactions from the last week of December.

❑ Pull an open invoice report and clear out any old invoices that are not accurate. Remember, deleting an invoice should be done only the company is on a cash basis, not accrual. It will affect the tax return if you delete or change any invoice if the client files by the accrual basis!

❑ Pull an unpaid-bills report to see if any bills need to be deleted. Again, remember the rule on cash/accrual basis.

❑ The P & L should show gross wages, not net. This helps match financial statements with payroll reports.

❑ The P & L should separate officer gross wages from employee gross wages.

❑ Verify that the owner has not made any deposits to the business bank account. If so, show the deposit as a loan for corporations or equity for a sole proprietor. You can also show the money deposited from a sole proprietor to offset owner's draw.

❑ Check for eligible 1099 vendors and process the forms by January 31st.

❑ If a company has more than one vehicle, the vehicles need to be listed separately, showing gas, insurance, repairs and registration.

❑ When everything is clean, set the closing-date password.

❑ When done, make a backup of the file.

Favorite Quotes

The successful person makes a habit of doing what the failing person doesn't like to do.

—*Thomas Edison*

Fall seven times, stand up eight.

—*Japanese Proverb*

All I am, or can be, I owe to my angel mother.

—*Abraham Lincoln*

Stop asking God to bless your work. Rather, thank Him for allowing you to be a part of His work.

—*Toby Mac*

Change your thoughts and change your world.

—*Norman Vincent Peale*

The time to repair the roof is when the sun is shining.

—*John F. Kennedy*

I cannot live without books.

—*Thomas Jefferson*

Tell me and I forget. Teach me and I remember. Involve me and I learn.

—*Benjamin Franklin*

God has not called you to be successful. He has called you to be obedient.

—*Darrell Scott*

The best time to plant a shade tree was 20 years ago. The next best time is today.

—*African Proverb*

What separates the winners from the losers is how a person reacts to each new twist of fate.

—*Donald Trump*

No matter how busy you are, you must take time to make the other person feel important.

—*Mary Kay Ash*

Risk comes from not knowing what you're doing.

—*Warren Buffett*

The growth and development of people is the highest calling of leadership.

—*Harvey S. Firestone*

I hire people brighter than me and then I get out of their way.

—*Lee Iacocca*

The quality of a leader is reflected in the standards they set for themselves.

—*Ray Kroc*

Knowledge is like climbing a mountain; the higher you reach, the more you can see and appreciate.

—*Anonymous*

There is more treasure in books than in all the pirate's loot on Treasure Island.

—*Walt Disney*

The most important thing about a goal is having one.
—*Geoffry Abert*

Therefore if you have not been faithful in the use of worldly wealth, who will entrust the true riches to you?
—*Luke 16:11*

Some people want it to happen, some wish it would happen and others make it happen.
—*Michael Jordan*

Love doesn't make the world go 'round, love is what makes the ride worthwhile.
—*Elizabeth Barrett Browning*

Many receive advice, only the wise profit from it.
—*Publilius Syrus*

Courage is not the absence of fear, but rather the judgment that something else is more important than fear.
—*Ambrose Redmoon*

Choose a job you love and you will never have to work a day in your life.
—*Confucius*

Steady plodding brings prosperity. Hasty speculation brings poverty.
—*Proverbs 21:5*

Quality is remembered long after the price is forgotten.
—*Gucci*

For me, life is continuously being hungry. The meaning of life is not simply to exist, to survive, but to move ahead, to go up, to achieve, to conquer.
—*Arnold Schwarzenegger*

Time is our most precious asset; we should invest it wisely.
　　—*Michael Levy*

Failure will never overtake me if my determination to succeed is strong enough.
　　—*Og Mandino*

The journey is the reward.
　　—*Chinese Proverb*

Our character is what we do when we think no one is looking.
　　—*H. Jackson Brown Jr.*

It's easy to make a buck. It's a lot tougher to make a difference.
　　—*Tom Brokaw*

Good, better, best; never let it rest till your good is better and your better is best.
　　—*Unknown*

If you have much, give of your wealth; if you have little, give of your heart.
　　—*Arabian Proverb*

Our talents are the gift that God gives to us. What we make of our talents is our gift back to God.
　　—*Leo Buscaglia*

What comes out of your mouth is determined by what goes into your mind.
　　—*Zig Ziglar*

Suggested Readings

When I was growing up, I did not like to read. However, when I became a business owner, something changed. There was so much to learn. I became hungry to grow and understand.

Below is a list of books that I suggest every CEO read.

✓ *Developing the Leader Within You* by John C. Maxwell

✓ *Don't Let the IRS Destroy Your Small Business* by Michael Savage

✓ *Good to Great* by Jim Collins

✓ *Raving Fans* by Ken Blanchard

✓ *Rich Dad, Poor Dad* by Robert Kiyosaki

✓ *The Art of War for Managers* by Gerald A. Michaelson

✓ *The E-Myth Revisited* by Michael E. Gerber

✓ *The On Purpose Business* by Kevin W. McCarthy

✓ *The On Purpose Person* by Kevin W. McCarthy

✓ *The Richest Man in Babylon* by George S. Clason

✓ *Your Money Counts* by Howard Dayton

About the Author

Renee Daggett, Certified QuickBooks Consultant with Intuit and The Sleeter Group, is the founder and President of Administrative Bookkeeping Co., Inc. She received a bachelor's degree from San Jose State University in 1989.

Renee is also a registered tax preparer. With this license, she uniquely brings peace to her clients by helping them with all the aspects of running a business.

Renee also has been certified as a budget coach with Crown Financial Ministries since 2004.

Renee has corporate financial management experience dating back to 1995 and is passionate about equipping business owners with the tools they need to run their business simply and efficiently.

Renee works with her clients to cleanse their financial statements, use QuickBooks, maximize tax deductions, reconcile bank statements, manage payroll, establish job costing, prepare corporate minutes and eliminate debt.

Because education is important to her, Renee teaches QuickBooks classes for beginners and a QuickBooks class specifically for real estate investors and property managers. Her company, Administrative Bookkeeping frequently hosts teleseminars in a conference-call setting that provide business owners and managers with the tools that help them succeed.

Born and raised in California and happily married since 1990, Renee is the mother of two sons. She lives her life with purpose and thrives on helping her clients do so as well.

You can learn more about Administrative Bookkeeping Co, Inc at www.adminbooks.com and contact Renee at 1-888-459-1110 or info@adminbooks.com.

Spread the Word!

Additional copies of *Your Financial Flight Plan* are available:

Fax book orders to: 1-888-459-1117
Telephone orders: 1-888-459-1110. Have your credit card ready.
Email orders: inquiry@yourfinancialflightplan.com

Each book is $19.95 plus any applicable sales tax and $2.50 shipping fees.

Payment methods: Checks payable to Admin Books or credit card payments accepted.

Check One: ❑ Visa ❑ MasterCard ❑ Discover ❑ American Express

Expiration Date _____ Validation Code _____ Phone_____

Cardholder's Signature _____

Printed Name_____

Cardholder's Address_____

City _____ State _____ Zip_____ Quantity ___

Email Address_____

Please send more FREE information:

✓ E-newsletter

✓ MP3 interview, "Business Owner's Common Mistakes"

✓ Half-hour phone consultation for prospective clients

✓ Year End checklist

✓ QuickBooks class schedule

✓ Speaking/seminars

If you have enjoyed this book, we would like to have you tell us the best part. Please contact us at:

Admin Books
1-888-459-1110
www.yourfinancialflightplan.com
inquiry@yourfinancialflightplan.com

Printed in the United States
204705BV00007B/22-84/P